BASIC SPIRITUAL DISCIPLINES

Scott Parkison

Shepherd's Voice Publishing

BASIC SPIRITUAL DISCIPLINES

Scott Parkison

© 2024 Shepherd's Voice Publishing.

All rights reserved. No part of this publication may be reproduced, stored in a retrieval system or transmited in any form or by any means, electronic, mechanical, photocopying, recording or otherwise without the prior permision of the publisher or in accordance with the provisions of the Copyright, Designs and Patents Act 1988 or under the terms of any licence permitting limited copying issued by the Copyright Licensing Angency.

Published by:
Shepherd's Voice Publishing
327 West Stevens Street
Cookeville, 38501 TN, USA

Cover Design: Andy Hammond

A CIP record for this book is available from the Library of Congress Cataloging-in-Publication Data

ISBN-13: 979-8-218-51476-1

Printed in USA

Acknowledgments

This book was edited, designed, and published by the staff and members of Stevens Street Baptist Church. It is a summary of a sermon series I preached in the fall of 2023. At the completion of the series, I began looking for a resource I could provide to new members of our congregation that would be a basic introduction to spiritual disciplines. I wanted something short and un-intimidating to a new believer. I wrote this book primarily because I could not find a book about spiritual disciplines that was short, concise, and formatted in a simple manner. I am thankful for the many people who helped get this book completed. First: To the members of Stevens Street Baptist Church, no pastor has ever had a better congregation. I suppose every pastor should feel this way about his people, but I truly believe I am especially blessed to be called your pastor. You have blessed me and my family in more ways than you will ever know. I hope this little book will be an encouragement to you. After all, you are the ones that made the writing of this book possible. To Kelly and the kids: Writing a small book would be a small task for a seasoned author. But for me it was not easy. Thank you for tolerating my absences on my days off as I wrote this book. Even though I was at home, my attention was periodically diverted towards my computer for several months. Whatever blessings the contents of this book brings to God's people, certainly you deserve some credit. To Katrina Leung, Jennifer Fields, and Ashley Michael: Thank you for your editing and formatting skills. I appreciate all of you so very much for your sacrifice of time. I also would like to thank Andy Hammond, Worship Pastor at Stevens Street, for designing the cover of this book. As always, his work is top shelf.

Pastor Scott

Contents

INTRODUCTION 7

CHAPTER I
The Goal of Godliness 13

CHAPTER II
Solitude and Silence 29

CHAPTER III
Meditate on Scripture 47

CHAPTER IV
Praying God's Word & God's Will 61

CHAPTER V
Fasting 77

CHAPTER VI
Be Discipled 91

Introduction

MY PERSONAL STORY of practicing spiritual disciplines began in 1991 in a jail cell in Ridgeland, Mississippi. As an extremely rebellious 18-year-old, I had not lived in a way that was spiritual or disciplined. I was wild and reckless, living for the thrill of the moment. I was angry and violent, looking for a way to fill a hole in my heart left there from the childhood trauma of my parents' divorce. Although I had been raised attending church, I had no desire for the things of God. My desires were for alcohol, drugs, and girls, and those desires pushed me to make many bad choices. I would often steal from people, vandalize property, and act disorderly late at night among other destructive behaviors. The defining moment came when I operated a motor vehicle while intoxicated. This mistake, along with resisting arrest and assault on a police officer, landed me in the city jail of Ridgeland, MS. As it turns out, this was the best thing that would ever happen to me.

In that jail cell on January 29, 1991, I had a life-changing experience. As a scared teenager, I called upon Jesus and asked him to save me. Alone in that small room, I prayed a prayer of commitment to Jesus and told him I would follow him for the rest of my days. I really meant that prayer. In my heart I knew I was asking Jesus to change the course of my life. I promised to leave behind my sinful, rebellious ways. I wanted a new direction, a new heart, and new desires. God immediately responded to my prayer. The Holy Spirit fell upon me like a waterfall. For the first time, I truly felt God's presence. It was the most exhilarating and fulfilling experience of my life. I was changed. I had been born again.

I immediately requested a Bible. Birthed inside of me was an insatiable desire to read God's word, but I had never read a book before. With my previous lifestyle, I was a terrible student. I never studied. In fact, I dropped out of school after the 9th grade. Still, I sat in that jail cell and read the Bible every day. I could not believe what I was reading. My new heart gave me new eyes to see marvelous truths in the word of God. I started in Genesis 1 and read all the way through Revelation 22. In three and a half weeks, I read the entire Bible. When I was not reading, I was praying. It was three and a half weeks of solitude, silence, reading, and prayer. My life of spiritual discipline had begun. Even though I was incarcerated, I had never felt freer. Those were some of the best moments of my life—moments with God that have shaped me into the man I am today.

I tell you that story for two reasons. First, unless you have truly been saved, you will not be spiritually disciplined. Jesus said, "You must be born again" (ESV, John 3:7). The Holy Spirit of God drives your heart to the word of God and into the presence of God. Unless you have a new heart, it is not possible for you to sustain a life of spiritual discipline. Unless you have a testimony of conversion, all your efforts at attempting to be spiritual are futile. Therefore, I encourage you to ask the Holy Spirit to reveal to you if you are born again. Romans 8:16

Introduction

says, "The Spirit himself bears witness with our spirit that we are children of God." If you lack assurance in your salvation, I suggest you speak with a Christian friend or pastor. In addition, reading and praying through the book of 1 John are good ways to seek the Lord for assurance that you are saved.

Second, I write this book from a conviction that practicing basic spiritual disciplines is absolutely necessary to grow your relationship with Jesus. Although the Holy Spirit uses all sorts of events to make us godly, the primary among them is the consistent practice of basic spiritual disciplines. I believe so strongly in this that it is unfathomable to me for any Christian to expect to be godly apart from them. Certainly, it would not have been possible for a scared teenager in that Mississippi jail cell all of those years ago to become a pastor apart from the practice of spiritual disciplines. In fact, every truly godly person I have ever met consistently reads their Bibles, prays, and regularly practices basic spiritual disciplines.

Therefore, this book is an introduction to the basic spiritual disciplines. It is meant to be short and concise so that a person with limited experience will have access to a simple explanation. My goal is to help you make time with God a daily habit. This book will not cover all the spiritual disciplines, only four that I will call the "basic spiritual disciplines." These could also be considered "core disciplines" or "personal/private disciplines:"

- Meditation Upon God's Word
- Praying God's Word and God's Will
- Silence and Solitude
- Fasting

Other spiritual disciplines include: simplicity, stewardship, worship, evangelism, serving, and giving. These disciplines could be called "outward disciplines" because, in some way, they involve the manner in which we relate to our church community or to the world around us. Those disciplines are communal or missional. The four described in this book are personal disciplines because they are specifically designed for you and God alone. These four basic spiritual disciples are to be practiced in private, behind closed doors.

My prayer is that this book will encourage Christians to spend daily, intimate time with Jesus. As a pastor, I am often surprised by the number of Christians who do not spend time daily with the Lord. They are faithful to attend church on a regular basis, but they do not meet with God privately on a daily basis by practicing basic spiritual discipline. I have learned to never assume church-going people are privately walking with God. In fact, I often ask church members to tell me about their practices of Bible reading and prayer, and many struggle to answer. Some of them will honestly admit they have never consistently read the Bible and regularly prayed. Most astonishing is the number of church-goers who are heavily involved in the leadership of churches who fail to practice basic spiritual discipline. They believe the right things, live moral lives, volunteer in church each week, and even lead classes, but they do not consistently read their Bibles and pray. They may prepare a lesson or make plans to serve, but they neglect the most important aspects of growing their personal faith. This spiritual malady can plague even the most seasoned of Christians. There have been times in my life when I have fallen into a rut of "doing church" but have not personally pursued Jesus in Bible meditation and prayer.

Introduction

A legitimate danger exists of becoming involved in church and losing your spiritual life in the process. That statement may seem odd to some, but I have seen this happen in the lives of many church-goers and pastors alike. As a result, they often lack spiritual energy because they are not spending intimate time alone with God. They pour themselves out in service to the church but do not refuel their own souls through daily, private devotions. A natural drift towards complacency happens when we establish a routine of public involvement in religion but lose the awe and wonder of God that only a private relationship with Jesus can bring. Lack of spending private time with him leads Christians to become spiritually lethargic and unwilling to live on mission. Without practicing the basic spiritual disciplines, you will become spiritually lukewarm. Showing up to a church building once a week will not automatically shape you into a spiritual person. While the local church is a means of grace God uses to encourage believers, to rely exclusively upon three songs and a sermon to grow you into a spiritually mature Christian is a grave mistake. If you desire spiritual growth, you must be willing to do more.

If you are a new believer, establishing habits of spiritual discipline early in your Christian life is especially important. I hope this will be a good starting point for you. For those who have been believers for quite some time but have yet to establish a daily habit of spending time alone with God, it is not too late. There is a life with God you have yet to explore, and it is my prayer that this book will challenge you to grow in your daily walk with Jesus.

CHAPTER 1

THE GOAL OF GODLINESS

"Train yourself for godliness"

1 Timothy 4:7

The Goal of Godliness

BEFORE EXPLORING the four basic spiritual disciplines, we must answer the question "Why?" first. Why should we spend time alone with God, fast, pray, and read the Bible? What is the goal? After all, a discipline is an action or habit repeated over and over to accomplish a goal. There is no purpose for practicing discipline without a goal. For example, an athlete spends time practicing his sport and exercising his body because he has a goal of performing on the field. Or how about a farmer? Why does he wake up early every morning and tend his field? Because he has the goal of a harvest. The student attends classes and reads books because she wants to graduate. In every example, reaching the goal requires discipline.

So, what is the goal of a Christian in practicing the basic spiritual disciplines? The answer is simple: *because we want to be godly.*

Apart from a desire for godliness, you will not consistently practice the basic spiritual disciplines described in this book. Other words we could use in the place of *godly* include: holy, righteous, Christ-like, spiritual or sanctified. All of these are used in scripture to describe how we become like Jesus. The purpose of spiritual disciplines is to make you godly. When you were born again, you made a commitment to follow Jesus; however, it is impossible to keep that commitment without disciplining yourself for the purpose of godliness.

Perhaps you have never thought of spiritual disciplines in this way. After all, people pursue God for all sorts of reasons, some good (e.g., godliness) and others not so good (e.g., personal gain). It is common for people to attend church during certain points in their lives when they feel they need God for some reason. Perhaps there is a big opportunity coming up, and they want to appease the favor of God so that he will use his power to help them get what they want. Others may be facing personal crises and decide they need to pray about them so that God will "fix" their situations. People pray, read the Bible, and seek the Lord at various times and for various reasons and for all sorts of purposes. But the only goal that will keep us on track spiritually is the goal to become godly.

The goal of godliness is a worthy pursuit. Paul told Timothy that "godliness is of value in every way, as it holds promise for the present life and also for the life to come" (1 Tim. 4:8). The measure of drive you have for godliness will be the measure of spiritual discipline you embrace. If you are lukewarm in your drive for godliness, you will be so in your practice of spiritual disciplines. If you have a fire in your belly for becoming godly, you will also be this way in how you practice the spiritual disciplines.

I want you to catch a vision for the godly person Jesus desires for you to become. Psalm 119:18 says, "Open my eyes that I may behold wondrous things out of your law." I want you to pray a similar prayer. I want you to ask the Holy Spirit to give you a vision of a godly you. Then pursue that vision of godliness by practicing the basic spiritual disciplines. Ask Jesus to open your eyes to how he wants to change your character and make you holy. Change is what we are looking for. Change from being a person who does not honor God into a person who pleases the Lord.

Two Natures

One of the best passages of scripture we can read which helps to give us a vision of the new, godly you is found in the book of Ephesians. In Ephesians 4, the Bible teaches that Christians have two natures: a sinful nature (the old self) and a spiritual nature (the new self). The godly person God wants you to become is "*the new self.*" The Bible tells us to "put off your old self" and to "put on the new self." "Put off your old self, which belongs to your former manner of life and is corrupt through deceitful desires, and to be renewed in the spirit of your minds, and to put on the new self, created after the likeness of God in true righteousness and holiness" (Eph. 4:22-24).

The Old Self

The image of changing clothes comes to mind when we read these verses. Our goal is to stop being the person who does not honor Jesus and start living a godly life that pleases the Lord. The old self is the person we used to be before God saved us. The Bible teaches we were born with a sinful nature and that our sinful tendencies manifest themselves from a very young age. As we get older, our sinful flaws do not improve. Until we experience the saving grace of God, our sinful nature is in control of our lives. The old self is the part of you with thoughts, feelings, desires, and actions that do not honor the Lord. No matter how hard we try, we can never overcome these sinful flaws in a way that completely honors the Lord. The whole reason we call upon Jesus to save us is because we see our sin and we want to be rescued from it.

Unfortunately, the sinful nature does not automatically disappear after you are saved. The old self continues to harass and hinder your spiritual progress as you walk with the Lord. As a matter of fact, you must continue to discover parts of the old you that need to be addressed, or they will stunt your spiritual growth. It is imperative that you tackle these old habits, attitudes, thoughts, and feelings. Like an old, ratty shirt, they must be cast aside.

You probably already know specific areas of your life that need to change and could easily make a list of your sinful flaws. If not, consider the compilation below from several lists in God's word: false testimony, anger, lust, adultery, retaliation, hate, hypocrisy, greed, worry, judging, rebellion, evil thoughts, sexual immorality, theft, murder, coveting, wickedness, deceit, sensuality, envy, slander, pride, foolishness, homosexuality, stealing, drunkenness, reviling, swindling, impurity, sensuality, sorcery, enmity, strife, jealousy, rivalries, dissensions, divisions, impurity, evil desire, wrath, malice, obscene talk, lying, loving money, arrogance, abusiveness, ungratefulness, unholiness, heartlessness, unappealable, lack of self-control, brutality, treachery, recklessness, conceit, or anything else that falls short of God's will. [1] The Bible clearly tells us to stop being this person. We must put them off, but we must not stop there.

---

1 Mark 7:20-23, 1 Corinthians 6:9-10, Galatians 5:19-21, Colossians 3:5-9, 2 Timothy 3:1-4

The New Self

If our goal is to become godly, we must then "put on the new self." The new self is the new you, the real you, the person you are becoming. The new self is the godly person you are becoming as you faithfully walk with Jesus each day and practice basic spiritual discipline. In one sense, you already became a new person the day you were saved. This is why scripture states, "Therefore, if anyone is in Christ, he is a new creation. The old has passed away; behold, the new has come" (2 Cor. 5:17). However, the new self must grow and develop in the same way that a newborn baby must grow and learn and develop into a mature, functioning adult. The new self is the person God is creating you to be. This is the godly you. The spiritual you. God sees you as this person. You also must begin to see yourself as this person.

Until you learn to put on the new self and walk in the Spirit, your life will remain broken. The goal is not just to stop doing wrong (*put off*). The goal is to be godly (*put on*). Godliness is not only what you stop doing; godliness is you walking in a newness of life. Godliness is when you "clothe yourself with the Lord Jesus Christ" (NIV, Rom. 13:14).

I recently repaired an old generator. It had a carburetor that was no longer operational. I removed it, cleaned it, and reinstalled it, but it still would not work. It needed a new carburetor. A continued effort to clean it would have never made a difference. If I had not installed a new carburetor, the machine would not be operational. It would still be broken. It is the same with you. No matter how much sin you get rid of from your life, until you put on a new self, your life will still be broken. This is where the beauty of the Gospel comes alive in your life. Through Christ, the thief becomes generous, the selfish becomes sacrificial, the liar becomes a truth teller, the angry person finds patience, the worrier finds peace, the slanderer becomes an encourager, the violent become gentle, and more.

If you are truly saved, your heart wants godliness. The struggle is attaining it. Although there are many situations in life God uses to shape us into his image, more than anything else, the ongoing, daily grind of practicing the basic spiritual disciplines will be the primary instruments God uses. Through them he will reveal to you the flaws of the old self and will shape you into the new self that is clothed in Christ.

The New, Godly You

Now, let's get practical. I want you to think for a moment about who you believe you need to become. There are some general ways to describe the godly, new self you need to become; however, Galatians 5:22-23 perhaps offers the most concise picture of godliness that applies to us all. Still, think about this from your individual point of view. What do you specifically need to "put off"? What characteristics do you need to "put on"? For example, while some people have no problem with patience, you may struggle with anger when things do not happen your way right away. Maybe you struggle with lust, lying, or a lack of peace. Many people find they need to learn to trust God more when the difficulties of life are heaped upon them. Some people come from a divorced home, have a history of substance abuse, used to be an atheist, or were homosexual before being converted. The possibilities are endless. What about you?

Ask the Lord to show you where your character needs work. The primary way we discipline ourselves for godliness is by making a personal plan for our growth that is guided by the Holy Spirit. You probably immediately know the areas in which you need growth. As you practice the basic spiritual disciplines, you will discover more. Do not become discouraged.

Journaling

As God speaks to you and as you discover the new self that he wants you to become, I encourage you to write down those thoughts. This is called journaling. Many Christians who practice spiritual disciplines maintain a journal to record their spiritual walk with Jesus. Keeping a spiritual journal is a wonderful way to record your spiritual goals and track your spiritual progress. As you practice basic spiritual disciplines, God will reveal himself to you. Write down what God teaches you. Journaling will provide you with a written record of God's activity in your life that you can refer back to when needed. Write down your prayers, goals, feelings about scripture, and how God works in your life. When you accomplish spiritual goals, record your victory! Set new goals and repeat. Record your failures, doubts, questions, struggles, emotions—anything related to your life with God and the new self that is being formed in you.

Spiritual Battle

Are you ready to pursue the goal of becoming godly? It will not be easy. Once you have firmly decided that you will walk the road of godliness, live for Jesus, and become Christ-like, there will be forces in life that will attempt to prevent you from accomplishing this goal. Basically, when you make godliness your goal, a war begins. You have an enemy. Three enemies actually. These three enemies are in lockstep in their attempts to keep you from becoming godly. They are your old self, Satan, and the world.

Battling The Old Self (Sinful Nature)

The old self will not be put off easily. It is still at work in you attempting to keep you from becoming godly. The old self is not spiritually disciplined and has no vision of becoming godly. If you were an alcoholic before you were saved, the desire for alcohol will not immediately go away. If you struggled with anger, lust, fear, and anxiety before you were saved, you will soon discover those temptations will come upon you again, perhaps even stronger. This is the old self warring against your new self, attempting to take back control of your life. Galatians 5:17 describes it this way: "For the desires of the flesh are against the Spirit, and the desires of the Spirit are against the flesh, for these are opposed to each other, to keep you from doing the things you want to do."

Did you catch that last phrase? The goal of the sinful nature (old self) is to keep you from "doing the things you want to do" or from becoming godly. The difficulty in this war is that it is an internal war. You cannot hide from it or run from it. The way you fight this battle is to faithfully practice the basic spiritual disciplines. You will not win this battle apart from the word of God, prayer, time alone with God, and periodic fasting. You will be easily defeated, and the old self will regain control.

Battling With Satan

Satan will also be warring against you. Satan loves your old self and wants you to stay the same. Satan hates people, especially spiritual people. He cannot stand for Christians to begin to look and act like Jesus. The Bible tells us that Satan "prowls around like a roaring lion, seeking someone to devour" (1 Pet. 5:8). He wants to assist the old self in winning the war for control of your life. More than anyone else, he wants you to fail at becoming godly. He will tell you lies. Lying is Satan's primary weapon. He will say "you cannot do it" and "you do not deserve it." He will remind you of your past and heap guilt upon you. He will do anything to make you believe that godliness can never be attained. Satan would be content if you would simply be spiritually lazy. He does not have to completely destroy you through some heinous sin, though he would love that. He just wants you to be a moral person with some type of religion who never develops into a truly godly person. If you want to make him smile, just skip your Bible reading for the day.

The way you can overcome Satan is to consistently practice the basic spiritual disciplines. This is how Jesus defeated him. You can read about it in Matthew 4 and Luke 4. Jesus was alone with God, fasting, and praying. He quoted scripture to win the battle. *Jesus was practicing all four of the basic spiritual disciplines when he won the battle against Satan!*

Battling With The Systems of The World

The third enemy is the sinful environments we live in every day, or the systems of the world. Although God is sovereign over all creation, Satan has a significant measure of control over the systems of this world and the people who perpetuate them. He has created systems in this world designed to aid your sinful nature, and he has blinded the hearts and minds of people. The majority of people in the world do not know Jesus. At every turn in life, the old self will find ammunition to use in battle with the new self. The natural patterns of life have been infected with sin. All creation groans to be released from this curse. You will encounter worldliness everywhere: at work, at home, even at church. Worldliness does not lead to godliness.

You fight against the systems of this world in the same way as you fight against your sinful nature and against Satan—through practicing basic spiritual disciplines. Through them, the Holy Spirit will empower you for living in the world without being of the world.

Spiritual Grit

You are in a fight—a spiritual battle that will exist until you reach heaven. To win will require the presence of the Holy Spirit, but it will also require you to develop some spiritual grit. You will need to practice spiritual fitness and train yourself. Paul gave good advice to Timothy when he said to "train yourself for godliness" (1 Tim. 4:7). No person of prayer ever said, "I pray a lot, and it's easy." No person who fasts says, "It's no problem going without food." It takes work. It takes discipline. It takes grit. We must never assume there will be a point when we will be spiritually at ease. While we do not work for our salvation, if we are to become godly, it will take tremendous effort on our part.

Jesus never promised following him would be easy. In fact, he promised difficulty, persecution, and hardship. That's discipleship. There is no place in Christianity for a casual effort to become godly. Christianity is for people who are totally committed. Your desire for godliness must be greater than your desire to escape hardship, or you will not succeed. Consider Jesus' call to discipleship:

> *If anyone comes to me and does not hate his own father and mother and wife and children and brothers and sisters, yes, and even his own life, he cannot be my disciple. Whoever does not bear his own cross and come after me cannot be my disciple.... So therefore, any one of you who does not renounce all that he has cannot be my disciple. (Luke 14:26-27, 33)*

God's Presence

Here is the good news. You will not face your spiritual battles alone. You do not walk the road of godliness by yourself. The presence of a Divine Person is living inside of you, comforting you, counseling you, guiding you, and directing you toward the goal of godliness. Jesus never promised it would be easy, but he did promise he would be with us. Before Jesus was arrested, he told the disciples "'I will not leave you as orphans, I will come to you'" (John 14:18). After he was raised from the dead he said, "'... I am with you always, even to the end of the age'" (Matt. 28:20). Jesus is the best resource we have for becoming godly: the presence and power of Jesus living in, around, and with us. God is not in a far-off place hoping we make it through this world. He is here with us at every step. We are not smart enough, talented enough, or disciplined enough to ever make it without him.

A beautiful mystery surrounds God and his ways. Although we are required to exert effort and discipline, it is God who makes us godly. Philippians 2:13 says, "... for it is God who works in you, both to will and to work for his good pleasure." Ephesians 2:10 tells us, "For we are his workmanship, created in Christ Jesus for good works, which God prepared beforehand, that we should walk in them." Becoming godly is a joint venture between you and God. That is why it is a relationship. You do all you can do, and he does what only he can do. He makes you godly. I have never met a person who believed they made themselves godly. Even though they have worked hard to follow Jesus, all of them credit God for who they have become. He alone gets the glory.

CHAPTER II

SOLITUDE AND SILENCE

"... and pray to your Father who is in secret. And your Father who sees in secret will reward you."

Matthew 6:6

Solitude and Silence

CHRISTIANITY IS A COMMUNAL FAITH. We do much that involves other people. We gather together on the Lord's Day, fellowship with other believers, minister to one another, encourage and comfort one another, and use our spiritual gifts to build up the church. This togetherness is critically important to our health and growth as individual believers. It is not possible to be a thriving disciple without an ongoing connection to other Christians.

Christianity is also a missional faith. Jesus told his followers to "go therefore and make disciples of all nations" (Matt. 28:19). We do this by sharing the Gospel and sharing the love of Jesus in ways that lead to more people following Jesus so that God's kingdom will grow. To be fully obedient to Jesus, we must live on mission in a way that interacts with people in the world who need Jesus.

Although embracing a Christian community and living out the Christian mission are critically important, this chapter will help you understand that you must practice your faith privately for your faith to be real. This chapter is about learning to take time alone with Jesus and away from people, just you and him with no one else around or involved. This secret, private part of your faith is foundational to your walk with Christ. Your soul needs time alone with God.

TIME ALONE WITH GOD

The basic spiritual discipline covered in this chapter is traditionally called "Solitude and Silence." I refer to it simply as "time alone with God" or "quiet time." In many ways, this will be the most difficult of the four disciplines because it involves a rare commodity: *Time*. It is also the most basic of the four disciplines because it will be the foundation to practice the other three disciplines. Fasting, Bible meditation, and prayer will only thrive in the context of being alone with God.

To be very clear: you will not maintain an ongoing, fruitful growing relationship with Jesus unless you consistently spend alone time with him. Just like any other relationship, your connection to Christ becomes distant unless you discipline yourself to maintain a schedule that involves time alone with him.

JESUS SPENT TIME ALONE WITH GOD

Scripture repeatedly records people encountering the presence of the living God when no one else was around. Abraham, Issac, Jacob, Joseph, Moses, Isaiah, Elijah, Solomon, David, Ezekiel, John, Annanias, Phillip, Peter, Cornelius, and many others all encountered God. It seems as if almost every significant person in the Bible spent time alone with God and engaged with him privately in some manner.

Jesus also spent time alone with his Father. On many occasions throughout scripture, Jesus would slip away from others and seek solitude with God. Mark 1:35 is but one example saying, "And rising very early in the morning, while it was still dark, he departed and went out to a desolate place, and there he prayed." While everyone else slept, he withdrew to a private place to be alone with God.

To some people, the topics of silence and solitude are boring, unreasonable, impractical, or even depressing. However, in our culture this lesson of silence and solitude is more important than ever. Some of you may be thinking, "I am already so busy. How will I ever find extra time every day to be alone with God?" Statements like this are proof that we desperately need to slow down. Our society is busy, distracted, noisy and more preoccupied than ever before. Still, have you ever considered that Jesus was busy? He was busier than any of us and for far more important reasons. Regardless, he consistently and faithfully practiced solitude and withdrawing from the world to pray and to be alone with his Father. If Jesus needed this private time, we certainly do.

Us Alone With God

Jesus not only practiced time alone with God, but he also instructed us to practice it as well. He told us to have a secret part of our life that involved practicing spiritual disciplines when no one was around to see us - no one except God.

> *Beware of practicing your righteousness before other people in order to be seen by them, for then you will have no reward from your Father who is in heaven. Thus,*

33

> *when you give to the needy, sound no trumpet before you, as the hypocrites do in the synagogues and in the streets, that they may be praised by others. Truly, I say to you, they have received their reward. But when you give to the needy, do not let your left hand know what your right hand is doing, so that your giving may be in secret. And your Father who sees in secret will reward you.... And when you fast, do not look gloomy like the hypocrites, for they disfigure their faces that their fasting may be seen by others. Truly, I say to you, they have received their reward. But when you fast, anoint your head and wash your face, that your fasting may not be seen by others but by your Father who is in secret. And your Father who sees in secret will reward you. (Matt. 6:1-6, 16-18)*

These verses teach us much about having a private life with God involving basic spiritual disciplines. They also warn us about practicing our religion in a way that is external and observable without the integrity of a private and personal walk with God to back it up. Clearly, the goal is not to simply be alone. Instead, it is to be alone *with God*. This is why practicing the basic spiritual disciplines *while* alone with God is essential.

Before we consider the positive impact of these verses and how critically important it is to be alone with God, we must identify two mistakes people make concerning this topic. One mistake clearly stated in scripture is concerning hypocrisy. The other is not as clear in Matthew 6, but is still a common mistake made by some people who believe being alone with God is a replacement for being present in church.

Do Not Be a Loner

It is a mistake to believe you do not need other people to practice your faith. Being alone with God is not a replacement for attending worship at church. People in this category say things like "I do not need the church. I have a personal walk with God. I can worship while I exercise or under a mountain sunset. I watch church online." People who believe this do not truly feel close to Jesus. They will not admit it, but it is true. There is no such thing as a private Christian. The point of being alone with God is not so that you can exclude yourself from church and become a spiritual hermit. Additionally, watching a worship service online is not the same as attending worship, but rather it is watching people as they worship. In no way does alone time with God replace the expectation God has for us to gather with his people so that we can worship together and live on mission together.

Do Not Be a Hypocrite

The second mistake is becoming "hypocritical." People in this category wear a mask of righteousness that is not really true about them. They practice acts of righteousness in a way that others can see, but they do not have a private, personal, secret walk with God. The problem is not that they let others see what they do. The problem is that it is fake and self-righteous. It is this mistake, the mistake of becoming a hypocrite, Jesus warns us about in Matthew 6. The frightening part is that it is possible to become this way unintentionally. Not many people set out to become hypocrites. It happens slowly over time as we practice the external commands of the faith (be moral, attend church, live on mission) but neglect the private forms of our faith such as spending time alone with God.

As previously mentioned, there is a legitimate danger in becoming involved in a church and losing your spiritual life in the process. It is possible to show up at church every week, teach, lead, smile, serve others, give, pray, all while being spiritually hollow because you have not spent time alone with Jesus. In such cases, a person is simply repeating a religious routine void of a genuine walk with Christ. This is hypocrisy. Again, for most people, hypocrisy such as this is not intentional. It is a subtle drift away from the Lord in our personal life because we lose sight of our personal, private walk with Christ. In situations like this, the temptation is just to pretend everything is okay.

That's what a hypocrite is, an actor who wears a mask or a costume to look a way that is not a genuine representation of who they really are. What about you? How many times have you attended church wearing your best smile pretending to be okay when on the inside you have not been walking with the Lord all week? I am not suggesting you share all your deepest, darkest secrets with everyone every time you attend church. Nor am I suggesting you should stop attending church when you have spiritual struggles. The point is that *your relationship with God is defined by your personal time with him*, not your public displays of religious involvement. True obedience is the result of a private relationship with Jesus, not through following a public religious routine. Routines are important; nevertheless, your routine practice of the basic spiritual disciplines are more important.

Find God "In Secret"

In Matthew 6, Jesus points out three spiritual disciplines, two of them are among the basic spiritual disciplines outlined in this book. Jesus tells us when practiced properly, we find God. In verse 4, Jesus says God "sees" in secret. God can see us at times and in places where others cannot. When you pray to God in secret, he sees you. When you read your Bible, fast, help others, attend church, give, and much more, God sees you. Some find this frightening; however, we should find it comforting.

What is most comforting is not just that God "sees" but that God meets us there during these times. In verses 6 and 17, Jesus says that the Father is "in" secret. Do not miss that! *"In secret"* is a significant phrase. In a real way, God's presence is with us when we spend time alone with him. He does not just see us when we spend time alone with him; *he is there with us*, in secret, during those quiet moments, in solitude with Him. We are truly in his presence during these times.

At the beginning of this chapter, I listed several people in scripture who encountered God while alone with him. You also can be in the presence of God in the same way as people in the Bible. You may not see a vision like Elijah or a burning bush like Moses, but God's presence is just as real with us as it was with them. People look for God in all sorts of ways. It is in the secret place where we can truly find him.

A Calm and Quiet Soul

The following chapters will expound upon the activities of Bible reading, prayer, and fasting. These are the disciplines you will practice during your time alone with God. As you do them, you will find that through these times with God, reading his word and praying, he will nurture your soul in specific ways. It is through these times the Lord will make you godly and will help you to have a calmness in your soul. King David understood his need for a calm and quiet soul: "O Lord, my heart is not lifted up; my eyes are not raised too high; I do not occupy myself with things too great and too marvelous for me. But I have calmed and quieted my soul, like a weaned child with its mother; like a weaned child is my soul within me" (Ps. 131:1-2).

Calm and quiet are the *posture* in which you practice the basic spiritual disciplines, as well as a *desired result* of practicing them. This means that being alone with God cannot be hurried. It must be more than an item checked off the to-do list for the day. Hurry and busyness are the enemy of a calm and quiet soul. You cannot race into the presence of God and expect to connect with him. That would be like me asking my wife on a date and hurrying through it as fast as possible because I have more important things on my mind. For instance, if I am having dinner with my wife, but I am preoccupied with my phone the whole time, I am not really alone with her. It is the same with God. When you set aside time with him, you must give him your full attention. Calm and quiet are not what the flesh wants, and it is not what Satan wants. Moreover, it is not what the world offers. But it is what Jesus wants for you. Jesus told us: "'Come to me, all who labor and are heavy laden, and I will give you rest. Take my yoke upon you, and learn from me, for I am gentle and lowly in heart, and you will find rest for your souls. For my yoke is easy and my burden light'" (Matt. 11:28-29).

Hurry

People say the world is busy and moves fast. I disagree. Look at how creation works. A tree does not grow fast. A field of crops takes time to yield a harvest. Jesus told his followers: "'Consider the lilies, how they grow: they neither toil nor spin'" (Luke 12:27). When we are in tune with Jesus, we quickly become more in tune with the life God intended for us. Do you think Adam and Eve were stressed and in a hurry while living in the Garden of Eden?

In addition, God also does not move fast. He made promises to Abraham and David that were not fulfilled for hundreds of years. All of scripture is a testimony of God's unfolding plans upon the earth over a long period of time. Anyone who expects God to move fast will quickly become discouraged. The whole reason we are called to a life of faith is because God does not fulfill his promises quickly. We cling to promises of a future that has not yet happened and that we must wait for. Patience and peace are fruits of the Spirit and thereby qualities embedded in the nature of God. When we read the Gospels, we do not get the picture that Jesus was worried, stressed, or hurried.

Mankind, however, is in a hurry, a big hurry, for everything. Drive down the interstate, observe people in the grocery store, call your friend during work hours. People are moving fast and going nowhere. Their souls are not at rest as Jesus promised. The systems of this world are hurried and expect you to be as well. They adopt the motto of "lead, follow, or get out of the way." Companies offer products with slogans such as "have it your way right away." Why does Amazon have 200 million Prime members? Fast and free shipping!

A Satisfied Soul

If anyone could say they had a busy life with significant responsibility and stress, it would have been someone like King David. However, he did not allow the pressing responsibilities of his kingship keep him from having a private life with God. He said his soul was like an infant that had recently been fed and satisfied by the presence of God. David declared: "I have calmed and quieted my soul, like a weaned child with its mother; like a weaned child is my soul within me" (Ps. 131:2). There is nothing more stressful than an infant that is hungry and crying. Conversely, there is nothing sweeter and calmer than a baby that has just been nursed. Our souls must learn to seek God in this way and be at peace with him. This calm and peace will only happen as you consistently practice the spiritual discipline of solitude and silence.

The Excuse

Perhaps the biggest excuse given for not spending daily alone time with God is lack of time. In fact, it seems to be the main excuse for everything we do not want to do! We have inflicted ourselves with hurry by becoming too busy and preoccupied. On the other hand, it is only an excuse for spiritual laziness. We must use our time wisely, giving a portion of our time to being alone with God every day and practicing the basic spiritual disciplines. Scripture says quite a bit about how we use our time. Ephesians 5:15-16 says, "Look carefully then how you walk, not as unwise but as wise, making the best use of the time, because the days are evil."

If we looked carefully, we would likely discover all sorts of unwise choices we make with our time. Each year the Bureau of Labor Statistics conducts a time study for how Americans use their time. One recent study found that the average American spends approximately five hours per day in leisure activities (i.e., sports, socializing, TV). Of these five hours, the average American spends three hours per day watching TV.[2]

Perhaps you could conduct a time study of your own. On an average day, record the amount of time you spend on activities other than work, sleep, and basic responsibilities. I am sure you will find significant amounts of unexpected time. In fact, you likely have a hand-held device that keeps these records for you. Open your phone and see how much "screen time" you used yesterday. Now, look at your weekly averages. How much time did you spend on social media, texting, and internet usage? My particular device will even record the number of times I "picked up" or unlocked my phone in a day.

In truth, we make time for the things we believe are important. The real questions: Are we making the best use of the time? Are we making time to be alone with God?

The Reward

Get alone with God every day. Find him in a secret place. You will learn godliness in solitude and silence with him. There is a reward that awaits you. Jesus promised if we will walk with

---

2   Rachel Krantz-Keat. "Television Capturing America's Attention," Sept. 2018 Bureau of Labor Statistucs www.bls.gov

him in secret that God will not only see us there, but he will also meet us there, and he will reward us.

> *... so that your giving may be in secret. And your Father who sees in secret will **reward you** (emphasis mine). ... But when you pray, go into your room and shut the door and pray to your Father who is in secret. And your Father who sees in secret will reward you ... that your fasting may not be seen by others but by your Father who is in secret. And your Father who sees in secret will **reward you** (emphasis mine). (Matt. 6:4, 6, 18)*

Three times Jesus promised rewards if we will practice spiritual disciples while alone with God. What is this reward Jesus promises? He does not tell us plainly; we can only make assumptions. Still, we can be sure it is something we will enjoy very much. Just like when parents plan something special for their children and when they are ready to reveal it, they will say, "I have a surprise for you." In the same way, God has a blessing in store for us when we spend time alone with him. I encourage you to go and claim your reward!

Where, When, and How Long

To be successful in spending time alone with God, you will need to plan carefully. There will be routine times of being alone with God daily, spontaneous times of being alone with God, and extended times of being alone with God.

A daily routine of being alone with God ideally should happen at the same time and at the same place every day. When I was younger, nighttime was best. As I have aged, morning times are the best times for me to be alone with God. Pick the time and the place where you can have the least number of distractions. It needs to be at a time and in a place where you are uninterrupted and undistracted. Do not combine this alone time with another activity. I often hear people say they spend time with God while hunting, running, or driving. When you are alone with God, you need to completely withdraw and place your exclusive focus upon him. Do not attempt to spiritually multitask. As for frequency, your goal is to be alone with God every day. However, if you spend quality time alone with God three to five days a week, every week, you are doing well.

You will also discover that there are spontaneous times to be alone with God. These are times through the day when God places his hand upon your shoulder and calls you to come away with him for a moment or two. For instance, when a meeting at work ends early, take time to step aside for five minutes and consider the goodness of God. Perhaps recall a scripture you read that morning, and whisper a prayer. These moments can calibrate your day, quiet your soul, and prepare you to face the rest of the day with confidence that you are abiding in Christ even while performing your daily responsibilities.

You should also consider planning extended times of being alone with God. I recently reserved a very small island at a local lake. I rented a boat, traveled to the island, and spent three days fasting, praying, and reading scripture while in complete solitude with God. I was able to practice all four of the basic spiritual disciplines for three whole days. It had a shaping influence upon my life that will never be forgotten. Even a half day schedule of solitude with God would be extremely beneficial to you. These times will be infrequent. Many people cannot spend an entire day away from their responsibilities on a regular basis. Still, if you are willing to plan an extended time with him, it will have a significant impact upon your life.

Your soul needs time alone with God.

Chapter III

Meditate on Scripture

"This Book of the Law shall not depart from your mouth, but you shall meditate on it day and night, so that you may be careful to do according to all that is written in it. For them you will make your way prosperous, and then you will have good success."

Joshua 1:8

Meditate on Scripture

NOW THAT THE IMPORTANCE of spending time alone with God in silence and solitude has been established, we must discuss the activities to place within this alone time to achieve our goal of becoming godly. What do we do while we are alone with God? Silence and solitude may sound relaxing, but the goal is godliness. This goal cannot be accomplished apart from reading and meditating upon scripture. Reading, studying, and applying scripture are foundational to all spiritual disciplines.

In this chapter, the terms "Bible," "scripture," "God's word," and "word of God" will be used synonymously, referring *exclusively* to the 66 books of the Christian Bible, both Old and New Testaments. The Holy Spirit has provided no greater resource than the written words of scripture whereby we might know God and become godly. Every spiritual discipline must involve the word of God in order to reach mature Christian discipleship. Unless there is a constant intake of scripture, you cannot properly pray, fast, worship, serve, or discover God's will for your life.

Much has been written and preached about the importance of God's word. Reading, studying, and memorizing scripture are critically important for Christians in their pursuit of godliness.

However, reading the Bible is not enough. We must meditate upon God's word for it to truly saturate our souls and change our lives.

Perhaps you were taught to read, listen, and obey God's word but have never been taught to meditate upon it. One reason Christians might not benefit from reading the Bible is that they do not read with the purpose of meditating upon God's word. In this chapter, I will define Christian meditation, explain why it is important, and provide a simple process of meditating upon scripture that will eventually become a natural overflow of your daily Bible reading.

Pagan Versus Christian Meditation

Christians might not use the word "meditate" for various reasons. However, it is necessary to note the difference between Christian meditation and pagan meditation. Pagan meditation is embraced by eastern religions, such as Hinduism, Buddhism, Jainism, Confucianism, Shintoism, and Shamanism. This pagan practice involves posturing yourself to empty the mind and escape from reality. This is the very opposite of Christian meditation. Through Christian meditation, we fill the mind with God's word so that we can live in this current reality in a godly way. Pagan meditation is self-focused. Christian meditation is Christ-focused.

Extreme Concentration

Christian meditation occurs when we listen carefully, concentrate intently, and think continually about God's truth in a focused manner with the aim of walking in full obedience to Christ. Casually reading God's word or listening to preaching is a worthwhile first step; however, this alone is an insufficient path to godliness. It requires more effort than simply reading. Interacting fully with God's word requires extreme focus and concentration, or meditation. The Psalmist speaks of meditating upon God's word in this way:

> *Blessed is the man who walks not in the counsel of the wicked, nor stands in the way of sinners, nor sits in the seat of scoffers; but his delight is in the law of the Lord, and on his law he meditates day and night. He is like a tree planted by streams of water that yields its fruit in its season, and its leaf does not wither. In all that he does, he prospers. (Ps. 1:1-3)*

Meditate. This simple, yet significant, word describes how intently we must focus upon God's word. Interestingly, in Hebrew, the word "meditate" means "to murmur." Murmuring? This certainly sounds odd! In actuality, we meditate and murmur all the time. For example, one of my hobbies is woodworking. It is often a challenge to measure and cut boards correctly so that the end product is perfect. I must pay careful attention to be successful. I often find myself intently concentrating with squinted eyes and mumbling to myself, especially after I have taken a measurement in preparation to cut a board. In these moments, an internal dialogue happens as I pay careful attention to what I am building. Through deep concentration, intense focus, and some murmuring, I am able to accomplish the task.

There are likely examples of extreme concentration in your own life. You may not speak aloud, but there is an inner dialogue and focus as you concentrate, meditate, and fix your heart on what you are doing. It may not be a hobby that causes you to meditate. Perhaps there is a concerning matter that is causing you to be anxious and worried. If you are able to worry, you are able to meditate. Anxiety is also an extreme focus given to a problem. The problem fills your mind and weighs down your heart. At times, we all give extreme concentration and meditation to something.

People commonly create a habit of reading scripture without meditation. Many often read the Bible quickly and move on without a second thought of what they have read. This practice does not lead to godliness. You cannot "speed read" scripture and expect to nurture a relationship with Jesus. When we meditate upon scripture, it remains in our minds and hearts. This is why the Psalmist said he meditates on God's word "day and night."

Christian meditation is listening to God's word with your heart, not just your ears. Meditating upon his word fills the mind so completely that an inner dialogue begins leading to comprehending what you have read. You may even begin to murmur and mumble to yourself and to God.

Delight

Everyone meditates upon that which they love. Many people love the things of this world; as a result, they meditate upon those things more than anything else. If you inventory your thoughts and desires, you will quickly realize what you love most. In Psalm

1, the writer declares, "But his delight is in the law of the Lord, and on his law he meditates day and night" (Ps. 1:2).

Why do we meditate upon God's word? Because we love it! Delight is *a feeling of extreme pleasure or satisfaction*. Do you love the things of God? Do you love scripture? Delight is an expression of emotional and relational love. For instance, you delight in the way you feel about your spouse, family, and friends. The word "delight" could even be used to describe how you feel about things in this world. Everyone finds a measure of delight in certain foods and activities. Still, our measure of delight in God's word should supersede all earthly delights. It is the foundation of Christian meditation. We are to love God's word and delight in meditating upon scripture more than anything else.

If you do not delight in God's word, you will never meditate upon it. You cannot force yourself to love something. For example, I do not like spinach. I can force myself to eat spinach because it is healthy, but I will never love it. I do not daydream about it or look forward to eating it. The day may come when I will eat spinach, but not because I delight in it. Some people attempt to do this with God's word. They read it because they think it is necessary or required because God says so, not because they delight in it. Consistently reading God's word will not happen out of obligation. Jesus tells us, "'If you love me you will keep my commandments'" (John 14:15). Jesus is not attempting to guilt or manipulate obedience from his followers. Instead, Jesus is saying love, or delight, is the *motivator* for obedience. The power to follow and obey him comes from love.

If you do not love God and delight in his word, no amount of resolute, human commitment will make any difference. You must ask the Lord to do something supernatural in you. Loving Jesus and delighting in his word are the result of a supernatural work that God must do in our hearts. If you do not love the things of God, do you really love God? Jesus said, "'You shall love the Lord your God with all your heart and with all your soul and with all your mind. This is the great and first commandment'" (Matt. 22:37-38). Meditating upon God's word must arise from a love relationship with him.

Meditation Is Life-Changing

Do you want your life to change? Meditate upon God's word and a godly transformation will take place. In scripture, this is called "fruitfulness." This godly transformation or fruitfulness is discussed in the New Testament in John 15, Galatians 5, Matthew 3 and 12, Romans 7, as well as in other scripture. *Fruitfulness is the visible results of godliness in our lives.* An image of fruitfulness used by the Psalmist is a well-planted, well-watered tree. "He is like a tree planted by streams of water that yields its fruit in its season, and its leaf does not wither. In all that he does, he prospers" (Ps. 1:3).

If you meditate upon scripture, God promises that your life will bear fruit. This is God's vision for your life. It is his promise to us when we obey, love, and seek him diligently. When you delight in God's word and meditate upon his truth something begins to happen. When the word enters you, results pour out of you. We all should desire this type of life change. The book of James emphasizes this point:

Meditate On Scripture

> *But be doers of the word, and not hearers only, deceiving yourselves. For if anyone is a hearer of the word and not a doer, he is like a man who looks intently at his natural face in a mirror. For he looks at himself and goes away and at once forgets what he was like. But the one who looks into the perfect law, the law of liberty, and perseveres, being no hearer who forgets but a doer who acts, he will be blessed in his doing. (James 1:22-25)*

Years ago, a friend of mine called me at almost midnight to ask questions about a passage in Leviticus. He had been searching for answers and simply could not wait until morning to speak with me. He had been meditating and looking intently into God's word and in that moment his life was being changed. Nobody chooses to read Leviticus in the middle of the night unless God is at work in their heart!

When people begin to look intently into God's word and meditate upon God's truth, the changes in their lives become obvious. They come alive. Jesus said, " ... an hour is coming, and is now here, when the dead will hear the voice of the Son of God, and those who hear will live" (John 5:25). The writer of Hebrews 4:12 declares: "For the word of God is living and active, sharper than any two-edged sword, piercing to the division of soul and of spirit, of joints and of marrow, and discerning the thoughts and intentions of the heart." I heard a sermon once where the pastor said "get into the word until the word gets into you."

God Still Speaks

If you want to hear God speak to you, read and meditate upon scripture. Because we have the Bible, God's voice is heard by his people as much today as ever. For centuries, God's people did not have the written word of the Bible. Now, God's word and voice are more accessible than ever. Reading Jesus' words printed in our Bibles is an opportunity for us to hear from God directly because the Bible is the breathed-out, inspired word of God. The Bible is inerrant, meaning that it contains no mistakes, but states exactly what God wants you to hear without errors. The biblical truths are literal. Everything that the Bible says happened has actually happened. Everything the Bible says will happen, will happen. The Bible is infallible. You will never be led astray by following scripture. Following the teachings of scripture is always the right thing to do. The Bible is completely sufficient. Everything we need to know and everything God wants us to know is found in the Bible. So, meditate upon scripture! When you do, God speaks.

God Speaks Directly

You will encounter the living Christ as you meditate upon his word. God will speak to you personally at specific moments. The Holy Spirit uses the scripture to guide, comfort, reveal, instruct, and nurture your soul. I can say that with confidence because it has happened to me. In 1992, God spoke to me through Psalm 27 and called me into full-time vocational ministry. In 2005, God spoke to me through Ruth 1 and gave me permission to marry my wife. In 2016, God spoke to me through Ephesians 3:20 and told me to accept a pastorate at Stevens Street Baptist Church. These are but a few examples of times God has led me to an important decision. Additionally, there have been many times when the Holy Spirit has comforted, illuminated, instructed, and nurtured my soul. All of those instances, which are almost too many to count, involved truths found only in scripture and never apart from it.

Getting Started

Start meditating on scripture simply by reading God's word every day. This is the first step. Again, read it every day. Select a translation of the Bible recommended by your church and just start. If you do not currently own a printed Bible, I recommend you purchase one. Although most information is now digital, I firmly believe a printed Bible is the most effective way to meditate upon God's word because you will not read the contents of scripture just once. While many books are a one-time only read, you will spend a lifetime continually studying God's word. It is far easier to refer back to something previously read in a printed Bible.

I strongly recommend a cross-reference Bible. These Bibles are designed to assist in connecting verses from one section of verses to another section of verses when similar words and topics are used by multiple authors. For example, if you read a verse about faith in Ephesians, a cross-reference Bible will point you to other places in scripture where faith is mentioned (like Romans). This has always been extremely helpful when meditating upon scripture my entire Christian life. For example, I was recently captivated by Revelation 8:3 concerning the prayers of the saints being like incense before God. When I used the cross-references in my Bible, I was taken to verses in the Old Testament which helped me to better understand how incense was used in the temple. I meditated upon these verses for a week; as a result, my trust that the Lord hears my prayers was strengthened.

Many people often use study Bibles. Study Bibles not only contain a cross-reference system, but they also contain commentary at the bottom of each page. These commentaries offer a quick interpretation of what you are reading. Personally, I do not prefer to use study Bibles; however, I know many Christians who say that study Bibles are very helpful to them.

Many people do not know where to begin reading. I do not recommend just reading at random. The key is to make a plan. While starting in the first book of the Old Testament and reading through to the last book in the New Testament may seem logical, this may not be the best way to begin. I usually tell people to begin in 1 John. It is five short chapters, all straightforward and easy to read. Next, I recommend reading the Gospel of John. Beyond that, I suggest finding a reading plan. Many reading plans can easily be found online, or your local church may have a recommendation. Reading plans guide you through scripture in a systematic, organized way.

As you read, eventually you will be struck by some truth in God's word. Whether a verse, a phrase, or a story, something will jump out of the pages, and God will open your eyes and touch your heart. When this happens, *stop reading and start meditating*. Dig deeper into these verses and spend plenty of time pouring over them. Whichever word, phrase, or verse the Holy Spirit draws you to, study it, memorize it, and keep it in your heart and mind all through the day. Pray to the Lord about those verses and ask Jesus how you can walk in obedience to what you have read. Write your thoughts in your journal and return to those verses the next day, or perhaps for several days. Underline those verses so you can continue to refer to them. This is the essence of meditation. Do this and God's word will transform you into a fruit-bearing, obedient follower of Jesus.

Scripture is *not* easy to understand, interpret, and apply; *it requires discipline* to do so. While some parts of scripture are easier to comprehend than others, most of the Bible requires your focused attention to grasp the truths presented. If it were easy, it would not require meditation and concentration. Consequently, I believe that Jesus spoke in parables and sayings difficult to understand so that people would concentrate, meditate, and seek him. Furthermore, the book of Revelation was written purposely in a complex way so that we would take time to search for the answers. God has wrapped himself in mystery. We will never fully comprehend him or his ways in an intellectual fashion, but we will get to know him better relationally when we seek and pursue him by meditating upon his word. This method of meditation flows easily into a life of prayer.

CHAPTER IV

PRAY GOD'S WORD AND GOD'S WILL

"If you abide in me, and my words abide in you, ask whatever you wish, and it will be done for you."

John 15:7

Pray God's Word
and God's Will

TO SAY THAT PRAYING is the number one private spiritual activity among godly people in the Bible is certainly not an overstatement. Both the Old Testament and the New Testament contain extended conversations between God and his people. For instance, the prayers of Moses, David, Abraham, Solomon, Hezekiah, Hannah, Peter, Stephen, and many others are recorded within the pages of God's word.

Although many people in scripture prayed, there is one person that prayed more powerfully than all others - Jesus. Simply reading Matthew, Mark, Luke, and John reveals Jesus praying on multiple occasions in various settings. There is even an extended prayer from Jesus in John 17. I encourage you to read the four Gospels and make note of the number of times Jesus prayed.

In the previous chapter, we learned the importance of God's word when practicing the spiritual disciplines, all of which must include scripture as a necessary component. In this chapter, we will learn how to apply God's word directly into our prayer life. Reading and meditating upon God's word should always lead to a thriving prayer life. When a Christian properly meditates upon God's word and hears God speak, the natural desire should be to speak back to God in prayer. Since the focus of God's word is to reveal God's will, it follows that a desire to know God's will must be a primary focus for effective prayer, hence the title of this chapter. Praying this way is a better method than "praying whatever is on your heart." There are many types and methods of prayer, but praying God's word and God's will is the way Jesus taught us to pray.

Struggling To Pray

Although most Christians affirm the importance of prayer, many struggle to pray effectively. I suppose there are many reasons why people struggle with prayer; however, I believe the number one reason believers fail to pray effectively is because they do not know what to say. They have been taught that they should pray but not what to pray. Many Christians have been told that "you can talk to God about anything," yet they have not received a clear explanation of what the contents of their prayers should be. They have been told to "pray whatever is on your heart" instead of filling their hearts with prayers that align with God's word and God's will. Without understanding what should be the proper contents of our conversation with God, we will simply make up our own! The result of praying in this way is a never-ending string of requests for God to bless us and to give us comfort and happiness. When these requests go unanswered, people either give up on prayer or plow forward with an ineffective prayer life that fails to change their hearts toward godliness.

Personally, I find it comforting that I do not have to make up content for my prayers. In scripture, we have a rich reservoir from which to draw the contents of our prayers! Praying "from the heart" is only effective if we have God's word upon our hearts and God's will as our primary desire.

THE CONTENTS OF PRAYER

There are numerous resources available to Christians aimed at helping them to understand and implement an effective prayer life. To remain concise, I will only focus on the *primary* contents of an effective prayer: God's word and God's will. The goal is for these two spiritual elements to drive the contents of *every* prayer. While God will listen to "anything that is on your heart," true godliness will only happen when we learn to conform our hearts, minds, and prayers to him.

Think about the prayers you have offered to God in the past, where did you get those prayers? Did you make them up or repeat some phrases you heard from others? Or was your prayer a response to something you read in the Bible? Was your request selfish, only for your benefit or according to your plans? Or was the prayer consistent with what God has revealed to you through meditating upon scripture?

I ask you to consider those questions because it is possible to pray incorrectly. James 4:3 addresses incorrect prayers and why they go unanswered: "You ask and do not receive because *you ask wrongly,* (emphasis mine) to spend it on your passions." We intuitively know we cannot ask the Lord for arbitrary things, including those that are selfish, sinful, and whimsical. We should know that we cannot ask Jesus for a million dollars and automatically expect to receive it. We also cannot ask for him to help us hurt someone or to take revenge upon someone. While most of us will not ask God for such "wishes," many people often ask for things related to life's comforts rather than praying for God's will according to God's word. We sometimes ask God for things without considering if they are in accordance with his will. Prayers with correct content are necessary if we desire favorable answers from God. Correct content always lines up with God's word and God's will, leading to prayers that God will answer.

Answered Prayer

We pray because we desire answers, which is why we take our requests to God. We know he has the power to do what we ask. When we talk to God, we do not want it to feel like we are giving a monologue or being ignored. The wonderful promise from scripture is that Jesus has promised not only to answer our prayers but also to answer them in a favorable manner. Jesus declared, "'And I tell you, ask, and it will be given to you; seek, and you will find; knock, and it will be opened to you. For everyone who asks receives, and the one who seeks finds, and to the one who knocks it will be opened'" (Luke 11:9-10).

Jesus does not want to deny you, hide from you, or ignore you. He desires to answer you and give you what you ask, but the way we receive an affirmative answer is to pray the right prayer. *Jesus does not promise to answer any prayer.* Jesus promises to answer a *certain type* of prayer, one *consistent with his word* and *according to his will.* The way to judge whether a prayer has the correct content is to consider the manner in which God responds. Did you receive what was asked? Did you find what you were looking for? Was the door opened by God per your request? Imagine every prayer you prayed receiving these types of responses!

Ask Anything

There are three times in the Bible where Jesus said we can ask for anything, and he would do it. All three contain prerequisites that the contents of the prayers must align with: (1) his word, (2) his will, (3) and the manner in which Jesus himself prayed:

> *If you abide in me, and my words abide in you, ask whatever you wish, and it will be done for you. (John 15:7)*

> *And this is the confidence that we have toward him, that if we ask anything according to his will he hears us. And if we know that he hears us in whatever we ask, we know that we have the requests that we have asked of him. (1 John 5:14-15)*

> *Whatever you ask in my name, this I will do, that the Father may be glorified in the Son. If you ask me anything in my name, I will do it. (John 14:13-14)*

These three verses hold the keys to answered prayer. Although I cannot ask for anything I *want*, I can ask for anything: (1) *God has promised* by praying scripture; (2) *God wants* because it is according to his will; (3) *In Jesus' name* by seeking to pray like he prayed. Jesus' prayers were always aligned with God's word and God's will. Jesus never prayed a prayer God did not answer.

Pray God's Word

Before you pray, read scripture. When you begin to pray, keep God's word open. The Bible is your prayer book, your prayer guide; you do not have to make up any prayer. Donald Whitley has written an entire book on this subject.[3] *There is nothing that will ignite your prayer life more than the truths of scripture.* If we believe the Bible is the inspired word of God that provides us with the infallible pathway to godliness, it makes sense we would learn to formulate prayers based on what is in the Bible.

There are many examples of how to pray God's word. Perhaps a person is unmarried and has a desire to be married. They should pray for God to provide a spouse based upon what the Bible says about marriage. Instead of praying an aimless and generic "give me someone to marry," they could pray specifically upon verses in Ephesians 5. If someone is having a conflict with another person, they should pray over the conflict by asking God for restoration, forgiveness, and unity using Bible verses on these topics. If someone is struggling financially, there are numerous Bible verses about God's provision for his people. The prayerful possibilities are endless. Every relevant area of your life is addressed in the Bible. When we pray about challenges and concerns in life, we are first to search the scriptures for what God says and then pray in the manner outlined in the Bible.

Sometimes you may not have a specific request for the Lord because there is not a crisis or a major need that is leading you to pray. During these times, simply choose a verse of scripture from your daily reading and formulate a prayer. When you meditate upon scripture and the Holy Spirit has touched your heart, pray

---

3   Donald Whitley. *Praying the Bible.* (Wheaton, Ill: Crossway, 2015).

over what you have read. For example, let us assume you have been reading through the book of John when John 5:17 was impressed upon your heart as you read: "'If you abide in me, and my words abide in you, ask whatever you wish, and it will be done for you.'" I have written the following prayer only as an illustration of how I might respond to this verse:

> Lord help me to understand what it means to abide in you. I want to learn how to pray and to ask you for things that are according to your word, but I know I must learn to abide in you first. Help me to abide in you by spending time with you each day, even when I am tired and do not feel like it. Help me to abide in you by reading your word and remembering it through the day so that I might live according to your word. Today, I have some challenges ahead of me, and I know there will be many distractions which will tempt me to take my mind off you. Help me to stay focused upon your word so that I might live in obedience. Give me the grace I need to abide in you.

Learning how to pray this way will take practice. Keeping a prayer journal and then reading what you wrote back to God in prayer may be helpful. With practice, prayers will instinctively flow from your heart after reading scripture and will become a natural overflow of your daily Bible reading. Rather than struggling with what to say to God in prayer, you will eventually find there is not enough time to say all that is upon your heart. You will learn to pray without ceasing as you talk to God throughout your day because his word dwells within you.

Pray God's Will

God has an agenda, a plan, and a will. He is actively carrying out his plan and his will upon the earth. He is using his sovereign power to accomplish his will in his timing. No one is smarter or more powerful than God because he has all knowledge and will accomplish his purposes. Unless you learn to pray God's will, you will be frustrated in prayer, you will not feel close to him, and you will not receive answers. However, if you read his word and discover his will, your eyes will be open to the mysteries of God. When you pray "'Thy kingdom come thy will be done'" (Matt. 6:10), your life will conform to his will.

There will be many times when you are unsure of what God's will may be, but do not be discouraged. If you are seeking God's will through prayer, your prayers will be effective in leading you to godliness. If you are faithful to pray in this manner, there will be times God chooses to reveal his will to you. When this happens, your prayer life will begin to soar! There is nothing quite like being taught by God through prayer as he reveals himself and his will. In times like these, your motivation for prayer will increase.

Praying for God's will is difficult since our human will is often contrary to God's divine will. The biggest prayer mistake a Christian can make is praying for what they want with no regard for what God wants. When we are saved, we make a commitment to abandon our preferred path to pursue God's path. Confessing Jesus as Lord means we surrender our will and conform to his plan. We must deny our human will and follow God's divine will in the way we pray if we are ever to carry out his will through the way we live. How can you truly ever expect to *live* in God's will if you do not *pray* his will?

Denying ourselves in the way we pray is beautifully seen in how Jesus prayed before he was arrested. Jesus knew he would suffer and die. Like us, Jesus had a human will that had to be denied in an effort to pray for God's will. To be clear, Jesus did not have a sinful nature, but he did have a human will. Like all humans, he naturally enjoyed life and desired not to suffer and die, yet Jesus denied the natural human desire for a long life and comfort. Instead, he chose the cross and even prayed for it: "Then he said to them, 'My soul is very sorrowful, even to death; remain here, and watch with me.' And going a little farther he fell on his face and prayed, saying, 'My Father, if it be possible, let this cup pass from me; *nevertheless, not as I will, but as you will*" (emphasis mine) (Matt. 26:38-39). Jesus denied himself, took up a cross, and submitted to God's will in the way he prayed before he ever carried it out through his actions.

Prayer is the way you put yourself on a cross before God. If you cannot follow Jesus in self-denial in the way you pray, how will you ever deny yourself and follow Jesus in the way you live? God using his power to accomplish your will is not the purpose of prayer. The purpose is for you to submit your will to God's will. The whole reason we pray is to submit to him.

Prayer is meant to change you, not change God. Many people lose heart in prayer at this point. They may question the point of prayer if God already has a plan and knows what will happen. The goal of prayer is our godliness. If the reason you pray is to manipulate God into giving you what you want, you will not become godly. However, if you pray because you want to conform your will to God's will, your prayers will lead to godliness. God is not a genie in a bottle who pops out to grant wishes and give away free "stuff." He is our Lord. You are to work for his glory and his will, not the other way around. There is perhaps nothing godlier and more Christ-like than choosing God's will over our own, sacrificing ourselves for God and his purposes. This is how Jesus prayed, how he lived, and why he died on the cross. Therefore, we are called to be like him in the way we pray.

Pray Like Jesus

Jesus told us to pray like him when he told us to pray in his name, "'Whatever you ask in my name, this I will do, that the Father may be glorified in the Son. If you ask me anything in my name, I will do it'" (John 14:13-14). Because of these words, Christians are in the habit of ending prayers by saying "in Jesus' name." However, praying in Jesus' name is more than simply saying the words. Praying in Jesus' name is praying a prayer that Jesus would pray. It is only when we are praying God's word and praying God's will that we are rightfully praying in Jesus' name. The phrase "In Jesus' name" is not a verbal incantation tacked on the end of a prayer requiring God to act because you said the "magic words." Rather, to pray in Jesus' name means to put Jesus as the incarnate Son of God in your exact situation and pray what he would pray.

A Perfect Model

The disciples wanted to pray like Jesus. They recognized there was something effectively different about Jesus' prayers as they saw God answer him many times over. Because it is his will for disciples to pray effectively, Jesus has given us a model prayer that perfectly outlines the content of our prayers. Some people call it the "Lord's Prayer." Jesus gave this prayer to his disciples as a model and guide for praying God's word and God's will:

> *Pray then like this: Our Father in heaven, hallowed be your name. Your kingdom come, your will be done, on earth as it is in heaven. Give us this day our daily bread, and forgive us our debts, as we also have forgiven our debtors. And lead us not into temptation, but deliver us from evil. (Matt. 6:9-13)*

This prayer is not meant to be quoted word for word. This prayer serves as a model for *all* our prayers. Any prayer that matches this model will be a prayer God will answer. The topics contained in this prayer can be found in multiple places in scripture. Jesus told the disciples to pray:

- **Prayers of adoration to God**: "'Our Father in heaven, hallowed be your name.'" These are prayers of praise where we exalt God because of who he is and what he has done;

- **Prayers of mission**: "'Your kingdom come, your will be done, on earth as it is in heaven.'" Jesus' favorite subject when he taught was the Kingdom of God. He taught us that it was his will for us to pray for the coming of the kingdom;

- **Prayers of provision**: "'Give us this day our daily bread …'" Jesus cares about you and wants you to have what you need to survive. He may not give you all the extra comforts you desire, but he said to ask for what you need:

- **Prayers of restoration**: "'... and forgive us our debts, as we also have forgiven our debtors.'" Forgiveness is a big deal to the Lord. He has forgiven you. Multiple times in the Bible we are commanded to forgive others;

- **Prayers of protection**: "'And lead us not into temptation, but deliver us from evil.'" Jesus has promised to give you what you need to fight Satan and overcome temptation.

Your prayer book, the Bible, is filled with all of these types of prayers. These prayers are according to God's will, and we can always ask these things in Jesus' name.

OUR PRAYER PARTNER

I will end this chapter with one of the greatest encouragements imaginable concerning prayer. You may feel overwhelmed thinking you will not be able to pray in the manner outlined in this chapter, but you can. You have a prayer partner who will guide you in your prayers and lead you to truth and godliness. God the Spirit lives in you and is with you. One of his purposes in your life is to be present with you when you pray and help you to know what to pray. "Likewise the Spirit helps us in our weakness. For we do not know what to pray for as we ought, but the Spirit himself intercedes for us with groanings too deep for words" (Rom. 8:26).

The Holy Spirit is the greatest resource available when we need help with the content of our prayers. He helps us to pray like Jesus because he was sent by Jesus. He guides us through the scriptures and reveals the will of God to us. With his help, we can pray effectively. With his help, we will receive answers when we pray. With his help, we are able to pray God's word and God's will. With his help, we can pray like Jesus.

Chapter V

Fasting

*"I have treasured the words of his mouth
more than my portion of food."*

Job 23:12

Fasting

WE LIVE IN A CULTURE with an overabundance of food. Within two miles of my church, there are at least 20 restaurants, plus grocery stores, convenient stores, and dollar stores. In many homes, there are pantries with food that has long expired, but it is well hidden among the latest purchases. When we cook, we eat our fill and then place the leftovers in the refrigerator only for them to be eventually disposed of. At times, the amount of table scraps most of us throw away each day is more than a malnourished person in a third-world country consumes in a day. Most everyone who reads this book will eat their fill today, and more. Although the recommended caloric intake for the average American is between 2,000 and 2,500, we average around 3600 per day. Most of us often feel like we must diet and exercise and eat so much we avoid looking at ourselves in the mirror.

Most people in our culture are uninterested in going without food for any reason, even a spiritual reason such as fasting. It is unlikely you have heard many sermons which affirm the spiritual discipline of fasting even though scripture says much about fasting in both the Old and New Testaments.

Fasting is *not* an advanced spiritual discipline only mature believers can practice. I believe it is a basic discipline even new believers should practice. A high level of spiritual "fitness" is not necessary before practicing the spiritual discipline of fasting. Fasting is an important tool that helps you attain the godliness you desire. It accelerates your efforts in prayer, scripture meditation, and spending time alone with God. However, it will differ from the other basic spiritual disciplines because it will only be scheduled periodically. This does not, however, make it any less critical than the others.

Christian Fasting

A simple definition of Christian fasting is *voluntarily abstaining from food for a limited amount of time, for a Christ-centered purpose*. Christian fasting is different from other types of fasting because we do it for a Christ-centered purpose. People may choose to go without food for various reasons, but unless the fast has something to do with advancing your relationship with Jesus, it is not Christian fasting. Fasting for medical purposes or prior to a surgical procedure is common; however, the difference between abstaining from food for medical reasons and spiritual reasons is obvious. Fasting is also radically different from dieting and the practice of intermittent fasting, which is a weight-loss technique, not a process for spiritual growth. While abstaining from food for health benefits may be something many of us might consider, there is nothing Christian about these forms of fasting. In fact, I would suggest we not use the word "fasting" to describe these activities and reserve that term only for when we are abstaining from food for a Christ-centered purpose.

Additionally, Christ-centered fasting is abstaining from food. Many people choose to abstain from certain activities to more fully focus upon God. For instance, people abstain from social media, hobbies, television, sports, or exercise to focus upon God. All are good habits, but they are not biblical fasting. While we should not be too legalistic about this, in scripture the words "fast" and "fasting" always refer to abstaining from food.

Reasons To Fast

Christians fast because Jesus said we would. In Luke 5, the Pharisees asked Jesus why his disciples did not fast. He made an interesting statement: "'Can you make wedding guests fast while the bridegroom is with them?'" (Luke 5:34). In other words, while Jesus was physically present with the disciples on earth, there was no need for them to fast. They did not have a longing to be with him because he was physically present with them. Jesus then went on to explain, "'The days will come when the bridegroom is taken away from them, and then they will fast in those days'" (Luke 5:35). Jesus said his disciples *would* fast after he was gone. This passage was fulfilled in the book of Acts as we see how the early Christians fasted. Moreover, this passage continues to be fulfilled as Christians have fasted throughout history and will continue to do so until Jesus returns because we long to be close to him.

In addition, Christians should fast because Jesus gave us instructions as to how we should fast. Consider these verses from Matthew:

> *And when you fast, do not look gloomy like the hypocrites, for they disfigure their faces that their fasting may be seen by others. Truly, I say to you, they have received their reward. But when you fast, anoint your head and wash your face, that your fasting may not be seen by others but by your Father who is in secret. And your Father who sees in secret will reward you. (Matt. 6:16-18)*

Jesus did not say *if* you fast, but *when* you fast. He clearly expected his followers to fast because he provided instructions about fasting. It is worth noting that Jesus said similar things about prayer and giving, which we also believe Jesus expects of us. What is especially striking is Jesus stated that there is a reward from God when we fast. Some may claim that Jesus did not command fasting; therefore Christians are not required to fast. However, is a direct command from God necessary to do the things he clearly expects of us? Refusing to do something spiritually beneficial simply because Jesus did not directly command it will result in missing out on many rewards of the Christian life. The fact that God promised a reward to those who fast should be sufficient motivation for us to do so.

Longing For God

Christians fast because we yearn to know Jesus more. To have longing for God means that we love Jesus and crave closeness so deeply we can "feel it in our bones." To have a longing for God means we desperately desire to do his will and would do anything to be close to him, which is why people in the Bible fasted, including Jesus. They abstained from food to seek God passionately. David, Moses, Ezra, Nehemiah, Ester, Elijah, Daniel, Paul, and many others fasted because of sorrow, desperation, or longing for God. The people of Israel fasted to prepare for battle (Judg. 20:26). Moses fasted as he received the Ten Commandments (Exod. 34:28). Israel fasted while mourning Saul's death (2 Sam. 1:12). David fasted for his dying son (2 Sam. 12:16). Ahab fasted in the face of judgment (1 Kings 21:27). Daniel fasted before he received a vision. (Dan. 10:3). Ezra fasted because he needed protection and provision (Ezra 8:23). Ester fasted before risking her life (Esth. 4:16). Nehemiah fasted when he heard bad news about Jerusalem (Neh. 1:4). The Psalmist fasted when others were sick and needed healing. (Ps. 35:13). Pagans in Nineveh fasted as a show of repentance (Jon. 3:5). Believers in Acts fasted as a regular part of worship (Acts 13:2). Paul fasted before appointing elders (Acts 14:23). Jesus fasted before he was tempted by Satan (Matt. 4:2).

In each of these situations, people fasted because they were desperate for God. Some needed to hear from God, while others were in desperate situations and needed guidance from him. In some of these situations, people fasted because they were expressing sorrow over sin, whereas some people were in mourning and fasted to express grief. Regardless of the reason, we see in scripture that the motivation behind each fast was a desperation for God.

BENEFITS OF FASTING

From a practical perspective, there are many benefits to fasting. From my experience, the word "clarity" describes what fasting personally accomplishes for me, but keep in mind that everyone's experience will be different. Fasting facilitates a greater spiritual focus than my daily time alone with God. While fasting, God's word seems clearer, and it is easier to stay focused when reading the Bible. I receive a deeper clarity of God's truths found in scripture, which aids in meditation on the verses I chose to read during the fast. Fasting also helps me to pray with greater clarity. Because God's word is clearer when I fast, my prayers are more thorough and focused, and I seem to have a greater ability to express my heart than I do during my daily prayer time. I can pray God's word with greater effectiveness when fasting.

As you can imagine, this clarity of scripture helps to see life with greater clarity. Because fasting slows down the body through lack of calories, it also slows down the mind. An intense focus upon scripture and prayer allows the spirit to slow down as well. The mind and heart are not preoccupied with the things of the world while fasting. Therefore, it is easier to see the world from God's perspective and perceive life from an eternal, scriptural perspective. This clarity aids in achieving my purpose for the fast, and I begin to see my situation through the lens of God's word. It exposes what is really important to me in life and helps me to see if my priorities are aligned with God's. Fasting aids in searching out the will of God and finding assurance in my decision-making.

Obviously, this clarity should continue in my routine walk with Jesus when not fasting. Still, fasting accelerates my ability to concentrate upon God's word and prayer. Because of this, I sense a greater connection to God while fasting. Although I seek this connection with him every day during my routine time alone with him, I become more aware of his presence and power in my life while fasting. Since I have greatly reduced the distractions of everyday life when fasting, my awareness of God is greater. Perhaps one of the greatest benefits of fasting is the ability to see inside my own heart and discover the sinful thoughts, attitudes, and desires that reside in me. Fasting exposes my sin. Remember, we practice all the spiritual disciplines with the goal of godliness. Fasting is the same way. Fasting is a mechanism God uses to make you godly. When I fast, I have harder cries, deeper joys. I make stronger decisions, have clearer directions, and pray more fervently. These are just a few of the benefits I personally receive from fasting.

Planning a Fast

Fasting is a temporary, drastic measure; therefore, it is important that it be carefully planned. There are a few steps to planning a fast. When you follow them carefully, these steps will help you to be successful: (1) Fast with a purpose in mind; (2) Combine fasting with the other basic spiritual disciplines; 3) Choose the right fasting method. These three steps are critical for a successful fast. For the remainder of this chapter, we will look closely at each step.

Fast With Purpose

Fasting is very different from prayer, Bible meditation, and alone time with God. We do not need a reason for these disciplines because there is a standing reason to do them every day. With fasting, however, it is important to have a specific purpose in mind. *In every biblical example of fasting, there was a clear purpose.* Fasting is observed during special times and for special purposes. It is not scheduled and regimented in the same way as prayer and alone time with God. This is not to say it is wrong to set a time each week or month to fast. Some believers fast this way and say it is beneficial for them. For example, they fast one day a week, one meal a week, or during a season every year such as Lent. These types of routines are beneficial because they prepare a person for those times when something happens that brings them a desperation for God and need to fast with a purpose in mind.

What is a good reason to fast? This answer will differ from person to person. People in the Bible fasted to hear from God, receive guidance, express sadness, display repentance, seek protection, or request help. There will be times in life when you will feel a desperate need for God to manifest himself in your life and your situation. When these times come, plan a fast. Schedule some extended time alone with God by reading Bible verses related to your situation, praying God's word and God's will into your situation, and abstaining from food. You will find your Bible reading and prayer times begin to soar as you combine them with fasting.

Fasting and Other Disciplines

Fasting is not an isolated spiritual discipline; it must be combined with the other three basic spiritual disciplines to be effective. If you do not pray, read the Bible, and spend time alone with God while fasting, there will not be much benefit from your fast. You can pray without fasting, but you cannot properly fast without praying. You can read your Bible without fasting, but you cannot properly fast without meditating on God's word. You can spend time alone with Jesus without fasting, but a Christian fast without alone time with God is pointless. This is a major error believers make when fasting. After all, fasting is meant to help you to focus on prayer and God's word more intently.

You will need to plan a fast when you know you will have extended time to be alone with the Lord. Your daily routine of Bible reading and prayer must increase while you are fasting. During the fast, you will need to schedule repeated or extended periods throughout the day to focus upon God in prayer and Bible reading. The longer these periods of time can be, the better. In fact, consider planning a fast during times when you are able to alter your normal schedule in a significant manner. Attempting to follow your regular daily routine while fasting may not give you the spiritual focus you are looking for. It is often better to fast when you can get away from "life" for an extended time to engage fully in all four spiritual disciplines together.

Do not "go hungry" aimlessly. The two biggest mistakes a Christian can make concerning fasting are having no purpose for the fast and not practicing the other spiritual disciplines when they fast. You must break your daily routine and focus on God. Otherwise, you are just going hungry for no reason.

Choose a Fasting Method

There are three basic methods of fasting: a partial fast, a regular fast, and a total fast. Many people wonder how long they should fast. The answer to that question depends on your purpose, fasting experience, and method of fasting chosen. A partial fast involves water and juice only, but no solid food. If you have never fasted before, a partial fast is a good starting point. Many people begin with a 24-hour partial fast as a baby step into fasting. However, a partial fast can be sustained for many days, even weeks, because of the minimum calories being received through juice. Many people will plan a partial fast because they desire to do so for a long period of time, but need some calories as a result of their normal, everyday schedule.

The next fasting method is a regular fast. A regular fast is a "water only" fast and is the most common fasting method found in scripture. In a regular fast, your body receives no calories and the effects of hunger are stronger. Many will start with a regular fast lasting 24 hours, which means they miss two meals. A 36-hour fast eliminates three meals and is a true one-day fast. A three-day regular fast is a worthwhile goal. However, after three days, the effects of fasting can be felt with greater intensity. I have even heard testimonies of believers planning regular fasts for 21 days or longer.

The third fasting method is an absolute or total fast. No food or water. I have personally planned absolute fasts, but never longer than a day and a half or 36 hours. The "rule of three" states a person can last three minutes without air, three weeks without food, and three days without water.[4]

Check Your Calendar

Your schedule is important when planning a fast. If you are an athlete or work a physically demanding job, you must consider

---

4   The Survival University, "Three Rules of Survival". 20 Feb. 2024 www.thesurvivaluniversity.com

these things when planning. There may be an important family dinner coming up, such as a holiday meal, involving many people. Perhaps there is an important job-related dinner meeting and abstaining from food is not a viable option. You must consider your social calendar, vocational duties, and domestic responsibilities when planning a fast. Although you do not want to advertise your fast to others, there may be some people you must inform ahead of time.

It is imperative not to be legalistic. During your fast you may need to consume some calories because you feel faint and are not in a position to rest because you must finish your work day. Perhaps your situation changes, and you unexpectedly find yourself in a group situation or have an emergency with work or family. God sees your heart, not caloric intake. You can keep your heart positioned before God and complete your fast even if you must consume some unexpected calories. For example, I recently planned a 36-hour regular fast that was scheduled to end after I preached my last Sunday message. Before worship began, I started to feel lightheaded. Knowing my body, I made the decision to take a few gulps of orange juice so I could complete my pastoral duties for the day.

A Hunger For God

I pray you will consider planning a fast even though many believers do not actively practice fasting in our culture. In our worldly culture, it seems odd that we would go without food for spiritual reasons. Yet, if Jesus did it, so should we. If you are hungry for the Lord, fasting will increase that hunger. Jesus said he had an appetite for the things of God that was greater than his appetite for food. May we follow his example and utilize fasting as led by the Holy Spirit, as expressed in this Scripture passage:

> *A woman from Samaria came to draw water. Jesus said to her, 'Give me a drink.' (For his disciples had gone away into the city to buy food.) ... Meanwhile the disciples were urging him, saying, 'Rabbi, eat.' But he said to them, 'I have food to eat that you do not know about.' So the disciples said to one another, 'Has anyone brought him something to eat?' Jesus said to them, 'My food is to do the will of him who sent me and to accomplish his work' (John 4:7-8, 31-34).*

Chapter VI

Be Discipled

"For while bodily training is of some value, godliness is of value in every way, as it holds promise for the present life and also for the life to come."

1 Timothy 4:8

Be Discipled

I PRAY THIS BOOK has been an encouragement to you and will help you to practice spiritual disciplines in a more consistent manner. Regardless of your current level of spiritual fitness, practicing the basic spiritual disciplines is a necessary part of discipleship. If you have never been a spiritually disciplined person, now is the time to make a plan. It is just like exercise. Make a plan, set a schedule, and get to work. Decide when you will spend time alone with God each day. Adopt a Bible reading plan. Learn to pray. Plan a fast. I am confident that if you make a commitment to practice these disciplines, the Lord will help you. He will give you the power and resources you need to become godly.

One way Jesus gives us the help we need is through other Christians. Therefore, my last words to you as we conclude is an important one:

Find someone to disciple you.

Find another believer who is currently practicing the basic spiritual disciplines and ask them for help. Find a godly, mature believer, and ask them to train you in how to be spiritually disciplined. If they are godly, it is because they have spent a long time in private devotion with Jesus. They have trained themselves in godliness and have the ability to train you as well. You do not have to learn the basic spiritual disciplines by yourself. It is always easier to train when you have a workout partner.

A mentor needs to be of the same gender as you and someone with whom you can establish a trusting relationship. Tell them you desire to learn how to read the Bible and pray and that you desire to meet with them on a weekly basis. As you meet, share your questions. Ask them about their routines of practicing the spiritual disciplines, and learn from their example. Tell them what you have been reading and learning from God's word every time you meet. Tell them about your prayers and ask them about theirs. Pray together, even plan a fast together. You must communicate your spiritual goals and ask them to keep you accountable, including confessing your sins and struggles to them. Set a time each week to meet with them just as you set a time each day to meet with God. Since you know they will ask about your spiritual disciplines when you meet, this will keep you accountable to actually practice them regularly.

Most everyone who is a mature disciple has been discipled by another. Even though spiritual disciplines are to be carried out in private, this does not mean other Christians are not involved in training you. After all, isn't that why you read this book? Having a person who will meet with you on a weekly basis and provide face to face guidance is the best training you can receive. This is how Jesus trained others. Although he preached sermons to thousands, he also met privately with his disciples and gave them the individual training they needed. Most of Jesus' teachings in the Gospels do not come from his public sermons, but from his private training with his disciples.

You may even consider involving more than one person in this process. Perhaps a group of three or four people of the same gender could be assembled under a discipleship leader. Imagine meeting every week to be discipled with two or three other people and how much this could help you to practice the spiritual disciplines. To be clear, this is not a regular Sunday school group. This group should be specifically designed to learn how to practice spiritual disciplines. At Stevens Street Baptist Church, we call these discipleship groups, or D-Groups. The purpose of these groups is to train participants in Bible reading, prayer, and alone time with God.

The weekly meetings with your discipler must stay focused upon training you in how to practice spiritual disciplines and become godly. The primary purpose of a discipleship meeting is not to catch up on small talk. Instead, the desired outcome of these meetings is to be trained in godliness through practicing spiritual disciplines.

I am excited for you! The power of the Lord is with you in this. Now, let's get started.

Printed in the USA
CPSIA information can be obtained
at www.ICGtesting.com
CBHW020955231124
17912CB00010B/179